Embrace

SONEE SINGH

First published in Australia in 2022
by MMH Press
Waikiki, WA 6169

www.mmhpress.com

Cover design by: Jennifer Dinsdale
Interior design by: Ida Jansson

A catalogue record for this
work is available from the
National Library of Australia

National Library of Australia Catalogue-in-Publication data:
Embody/Sonee Singh

978-0-6454501-3-2(Hardback)
978-0-6451486-9-3 (Paperback)

For My Family
Who I was born into
And
My Friends
The family I chose
You are all in me

The pandemic opened me to writing poetry. It became a way for me to process what I was going through and what I was seeing in others. Rather than fight the experiences, poetry helped me embrace them. When I did, I realized poetry was everywhere.

According to Merriam Webster, Embrace means the following:

To cherish, love

To take in or include as a part, item, or element of a more inclusive whole

Embracing to me meant acceptance. Like the Serenity Prayer, it involved discerning what I could change and doing something about it, and accepting what I couldn't and making the best of it. This poetry was my ability to harness the energy of what surrounded me and grow.

The book is divided into 12 sections. Twelve is a master number that deals with self-expression. It holds the power of the force in all things and grants us the ability to manifest and to grow spiritually. Twelve is also represented in many cycles. There are 12 hours in the ante meridiem and 12 hours in the post meridiem. The outer rim of the Buddhist Wheel of Life or Bhavachakra has 12 links. There are 12 months in a year, 12 astrological zodiac signs, and 12 signs in the Chinese zodiac.

Everything occurs in cycles and embracing this truth, embracing that things come and go, that they have consequences, yet nothing lasts forever, is part of living. I recognize that everything that happened before led me to this place—here and now. I don't know what will happen next but I know it is already taking shape, and I embrace that.

Cycles

Celestial predictions that manifest on earth

Ties that show how connected we are to all that is

Guided by planets, animals, stars, moon, sun

The elements and so much more

How we come to terms with life

Change and evolution

How we deal physically, mentally, and spiritually

Showcasing our strengths and weaknesses

Highlighting our characteristics and traits

Depicting us for who we are

As we are

I

Where life begins

Self & identity

Self-consciousness

How others perceive you

Ignorance

Park bench

She cared

Deeply and genuinely

Listened intently

Saw beneath the surface

Same person

Be the same person
At work and at home
With family and friends

I didn't feel I could
Compartmentalizing
Slices of me

Based on judgment
I was less exposed
In my walls of safety

Nestled in my fear
Tucked in my inner world
Made me lonely

In search of community

Yearning for connection

I became a jack

Of so many trades

Dipped my toes

Until I found my place

All of me finally together

I can't explain

The freedom I feel

Personality

Calm

Strong

Open

And responsible

How some describe my

So-called personality

Intense

Meek

Flexible

And caring

How I describe my

Real-life personality

I am

Who

I am

And no one else I can be

Regardless of descriptions

Or despite them

Relevance

My issue

Is not

Annihilation

That

Would be

Obliteration

My issue

Is

Irrelevance

How can
I be
Significant

I am
One
Enough

That
Is
Relevance

Comfortable

Will I ever

Feel at ease

To look upon

My birthday suit

And not hide

In protective armor

Totally free

Spontaneous

Without carefully

Calculating

What it feels like

In my body

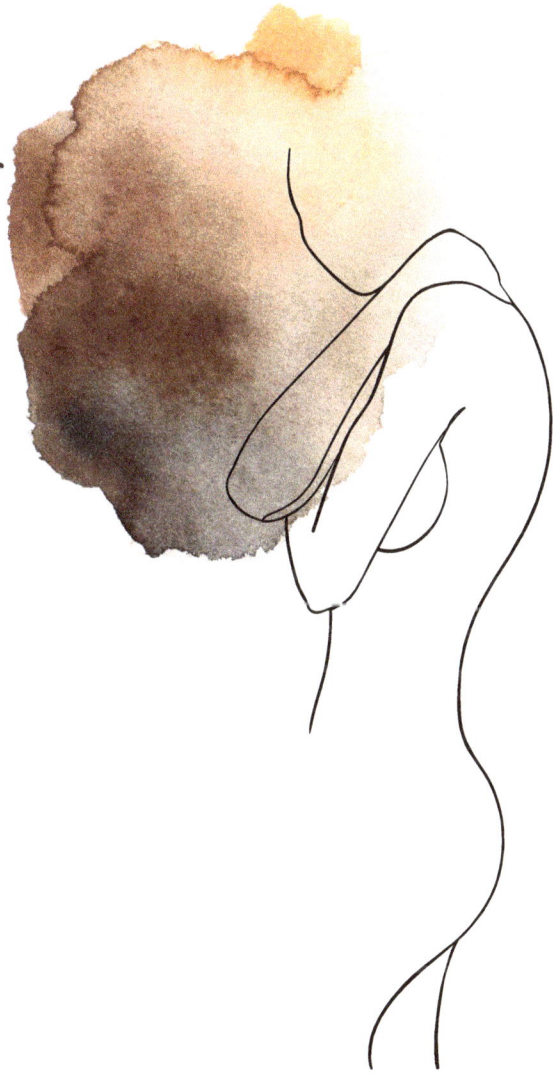

Who I can be

I can be no other

I cannot be taller

Have thicker hair

A darker shade of skin

I can only be

I cannot feel good running

Have a workout in a gym

Enjoy animals trapped in a zoo

I can be no other

I cannot always comprehend

Gains that broke my fortitude

Losses that made me stronger

I can only be

I cannot fake it

People who broke me

People who shaped me

I can be no other

I cannot stop feeling

Sensations that guide me

Hesitation that stops me

I can only be

I cannot help it

What I was given

The glory of me

Who is it?

Who is it?

The voice in my head

I hear it

It feels separate

From me

Where does it come from

If not me?

Who is it?

I sense and feel

I think and experience

And still

It is inside

And outside

Is it me?

Who is it?

It sounds deeper

Wiser

Experienced far beyond

Other times

Other lives

And this one?

Who is it?

The seat

The spectator

The consciousness

The awareness

Energy

Me

Naked

A body flashes
Through the window

She points confused
Are they crazy

She asks

No, beti

They are comfortable
In their own skin

She explains, covering
Her daughter's eyes

II

Value and self-worth

Possessions

Fresh responsibility

Mental formation

Sense of power

Treasure

Many feel what I have is of no use

Trash to them

Precious to me

Candles that marked birthdays

Corks that cheered memorable days

Handwritten messages on brittle paper

A measure of nostalgia I held

Forced to release

By movers who lost my box

Rising

I feel a gurgling
I watch it come
Rising from my deep recess

A cavernous place
The place that holds the bad and the ugly
Like Clint without the good

It steams up and bubbles
Like a volcano ready to explode
I watch the explosion

The lava launch into the sky
Searing splatting on the ground
Streaming down its path

Intense heat spreads
Hardening into molten rock
Eventually cooling

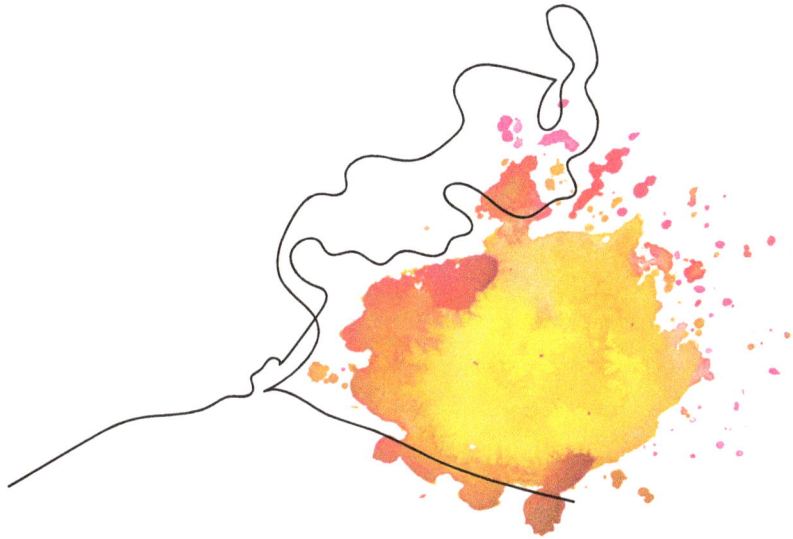

I don't become the hot rising lava

I don't simmer and bubble

I don't cool into hard rock

I haven't become it

It hasn't taken hold of me

I feel richer for it

I have collected another hue

One more stroke of the brush

Amongst the billion others

And I let go

That is all it is

All it will ever be

Enough already

Enough already

Plagues of self-doubt
Self-pity that circles
Forming excuses for
Laziness and procrastination
Barriers of fear
Molding of disbelief
Into emotional padding
Shutting down
Shutting out
Blocks of judgmental
Critical thoughts
Bridges that separate

Enough already

Resort to self-care
Self-love that is inherent
Forming support for
Abundance and action
Barriers to nothing
Molding faith
Into eventual surrender
Embracing joy
Embracing serenity
Blocks of healthy
Positive thoughts
Bridges to connection

Already enough

No place

Fear is a universal sentiment
Ailing our conscious and subconscious

Engrains and burrows
In places we cannot see

Rearing in sleepless nights
Falling hair and tight jaws

Inability to focus
Allergies, rashes, and acne

Sore muscles and headaches
Sneezing and coughing

Inexplicable phobias and stress
Sadness, depression, and loneliness

Bickering, impatience, and jealousy
More than or less than

The truth cannot escape us
No matter how much we struggle

Accept our universality
The eternal nature of our souls

We matter and we are worthy
We are connected and we belong

There is a place for us
We will not be destroyed

We are loved
Just as we are

In love there is no place
For fear

Fear has no place
In love

Worthiness

What is my value
If I don't value myself

Bending this way and that
Like oat grass in the wind

Turning in every direction
Like a sunflower in search of its light

Forgetting my own nourishment
Because I place it out to others
Without care of what I need

What is my value
If I don't value myself

Learning to root into the earth
A redwood standing strong

Growing tall into the sky
A flower blooming to propagate

Feeling the torch burning eternally within
I am the water, sun, oxygen
I am all I need

Natural state

I am

In my natural state of goodness

My body feels well

Gentle movement ripples through my soul

Allowing me to reach where I stretch

My mind is calm

Thoughts flow where the journey drives

Watching my adaptable approach

My spirit is at peace

Feels natural to master my will

Heed the calling of my heart

I collected all of myself

My inner fire is lit

I have fully stepped into my power

I am

In my natural state of goodness

Lift the veil

A blessing for you
For the year
For the decade
For your life

May you see and feel
How much you've grown
What you've learned
How far you've come

May you recognize
Obstacles and challenges
Were clearing the path
For something bigger and better

May your veil be lifted
The darkness disperse
Love is in you
As it is in us all

May the light within
Guide you
As it always has
Shining ever so bright

May you love yourself
See your worth
Your pure light
In all its glory

May you feel
You are loved
You are love
You are loving

You are all there is
Joyously at peace
Surrender
To the belief

May you recognize
Within yourself
The wonder
I see

In you
The beauty
You bring
To my life

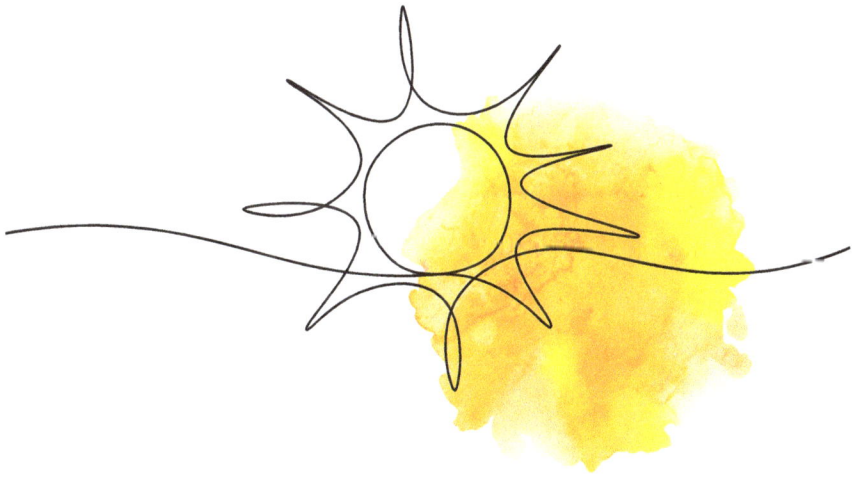

Land of dreams

It took me years
Of obsessive visualizing
It felt comforting

I lived in a land of dreams
That fueled delusions
Cocooned in the make believe

Pleasantly unaware of being awake
Creating incredible fantastical worlds
That never came to be

I will continue no more
That is done now
There is no more denying

I am eager to experience
Life in real adventure
Take a true journey

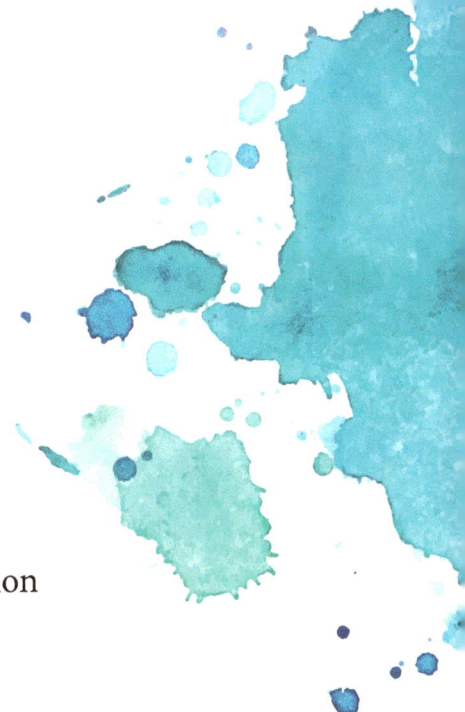

Cherish the moments

Attentive to what is present

Take a hard look in the mirror

This dimension deserves my attention

A captive participant

Rising to meet the tangible

Grab the horns and hold on tight

Knuckles turned white

Grasp the click of the clock

Where tales prick the skin

Activity creates soreness in the soul

Magic raises goosebumps to the spirit

Following the well-lit road

I finally feel

I have come into my own

III

Sharing

Communication

Education

Consciousness

Cause and effect

Nostalgia

Sometimes I yearn for
Times that passed

When we took time with
Hand-written notes and long letters

Pressing news took weeks or months
But for a few words on a telegram

Choosing what to watch meant turning the dial
To switch between two channels

Couldn't skip unless fast forwarding
A cassette through side B

A call involved a phone plugged to a wall
Waiting for a busy signal to ease up

Communication wasn't instant

Gatherings couldn't be changed in a flash

We made arrangements to meet

At exact hours and places

Slower times with fewer demands

Less at our disposal to play and explore

I don't always yearn for

Times that have passed

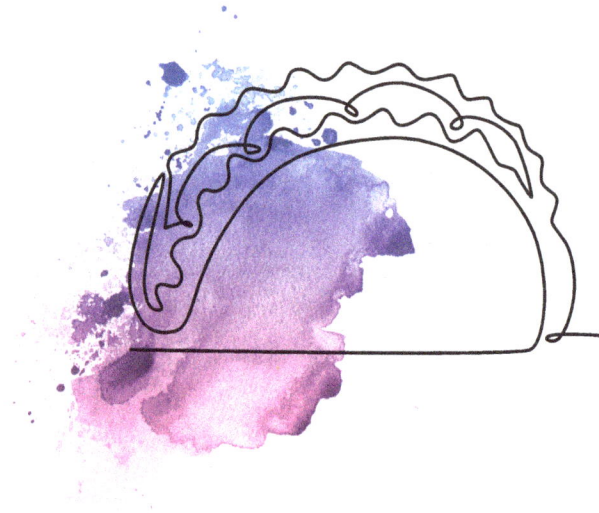

Silence

The half-eaten taco
Suddenly in focus
Its cold staleness
A taunt

Growing ever more limp
Fat coagulating with soggy salsa
Withering into the plate
Soon to be thrown out

The only thing palpable
Is the silence between
That wreaked in the air
Like day old fish

I know you better

I know you better

Than you know yourself

How is that possible?

You don't live in my head

Stay up with my thoughts

Hang out with my feelings

Seek comfort in my skin

Get overtaken by my emotions

Freak out at my plans

Panic at my to-do list

Fall asleep to my musings

Care about my desires

Wish upon my dreams

These are all things I do

How could you know me

If you don't know this

Nervous

I don't know why lately
I get so nervous to speak

I lie
I do know

I don't want to speak
About myself

What's coming or happening
I want to live it

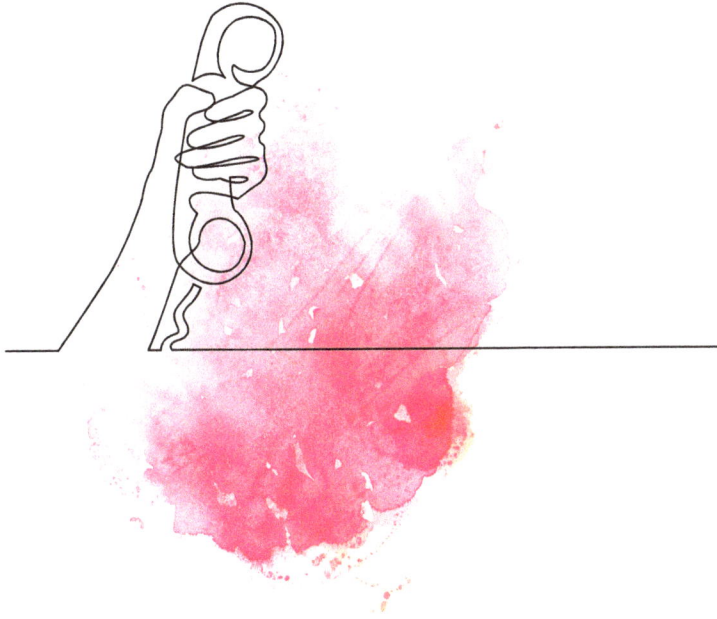

Not talk about it
Avoid the judgment and criticism

Stay small and quiet
I put myself on the spot

I don't need to do that
On the phone

Spotlight

I feel the heat rise

Break out in sweat

Nervous

In the spotlight

Can't wait

To be back

In peace and quiet

Ladder

Learning is like a ladder
Every step we take
We realize there is more
The higher we get
The more steps to go

When we feel
We have reached far enough
We look up to see
Steps rising steeply
Into the heavenly sky

And so I wish
To never give up
Constantly climbing
Up the ladder
Eternally a student

Listening

In lending an ear I sit

In sitting I quiet

In the quiet I listen

In listening I feel

In feeling I connect

In connection I open

In openness I give

In giving freely I receive

Heart consciousness

Manifest with the heart

Allow it to feel freely

Honor its true direction

Bring those who cause anger

Bitterness hurt and frustration

Turn pain to compassion

Allow what comes to surface

Release it so it will not come back

Without denying or rejecting

Work daily with spirit

Quiet the mind

Rest allows for surrender and flow

Time cannot be rushed

Accept it just is

Release the need to race

Things happen when they are meant to

Enjoy the moment

Rest in what is

Pay close attention to synchronicities

Honor that nothing happens at random

Measure success by living in purpose

Be courageous

No matter how small the act

Show up every day

Allow heart's healing

Healing to oneness

Oneness to love

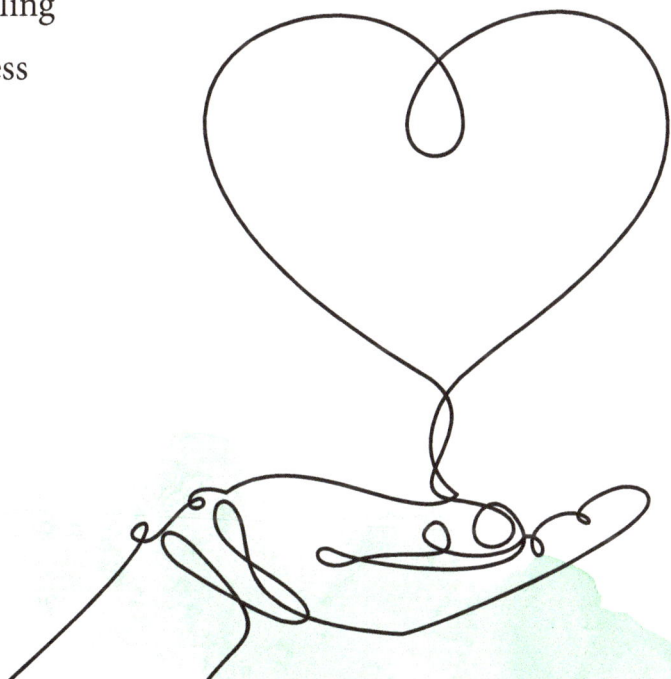

IV

Home

Family & Ancestry

Belonging

Conceptualization

Intellectual discovery

Past

Anytime we peer
Into our past
We risk finding hurts
We dug deep inside
Not to uncover

I have been told
Accepting the past
Is part of healing
Not just saying it happened
But uncovering it all

Bringing our past

Into the light

Creates an opportunity

To accept that what happened

Actually did

It stops to haunt us

Uncovers what made us

The way we are

It helps us find ways

To cope and to heal

Acceptance

Accept the past

Sounds simple yet key

To provide solace and peace

Release frustration

Disappointment and unease

We cannot change the past

Or what others do

Accept the freedom in being ourselves

Not what others expect

To conform

It takes courage to be

Unique as a snowflake

Only in community we become snow

Accept the generosity
A supportive tribe
It's even more wonderful
When mutual love prevails
Having each other's back
There is beauty in connection
That feels like home

Accept we can change ourselves
How we feel and think
Begin anew
On a different phase
Another starting point
Feeling less encumbered
And free

Grateful

I am grateful
Because of all I have
Fuels possibility

I am grateful
Because I am supported
Always hopeful

I am grateful
Because I evolved
Made it in one piece

I am grateful
Because I shed parts
Transformed

I am grateful
Because others came
When people left

I am grateful
Because of all that is around me
Here, in this moment

I am grateful
Because of all I have
And all I am

Moving

Aren't they amazing
The cycles of life

Arrive and settle
Starting with little

Creating our flare
End up with a ton

Imprint and routine
Become part of us

Yet in the farewell
We swiftly compact

Generic padding and folding

Monochrome containers

Memories packed

Into mere boxes

Years swept

In a matter of hours

Only to start a new

Cycle of amazement

Vintage

Scrapes and bumps
Create a worn look

Some call it vintage
Proud of its mystery

Others old
Ready to make it history

Ancestors

Grandparents of parents
Parents of grandparents
A long heritage

The unseen clan
Of my existence
Spirits of the departed

Ghosts some say
Lurking in my sphere
Prodding and protecting

All in a line
People upon people
Who came before me

Because they've been there

Seen it all

Have an awareness

I don't yet have

They know

What I can't see

They influence

Unbeknownst to me

Although at times

I do notice

Their influence speaks

Surprising me

Creating a legacy

I either crush

Or struggle to uphold

Maybe it is neither

Or maybe it is both

The ancestors in me

Home

Where do I come from
Where do I go
I do not know

Where was I born
Where will I die
I do not know

How was I created
How will I perish
I do not know

All I know
I am here
Right now

All I know
Is this time
This place

All I know
Where I am
Is my home

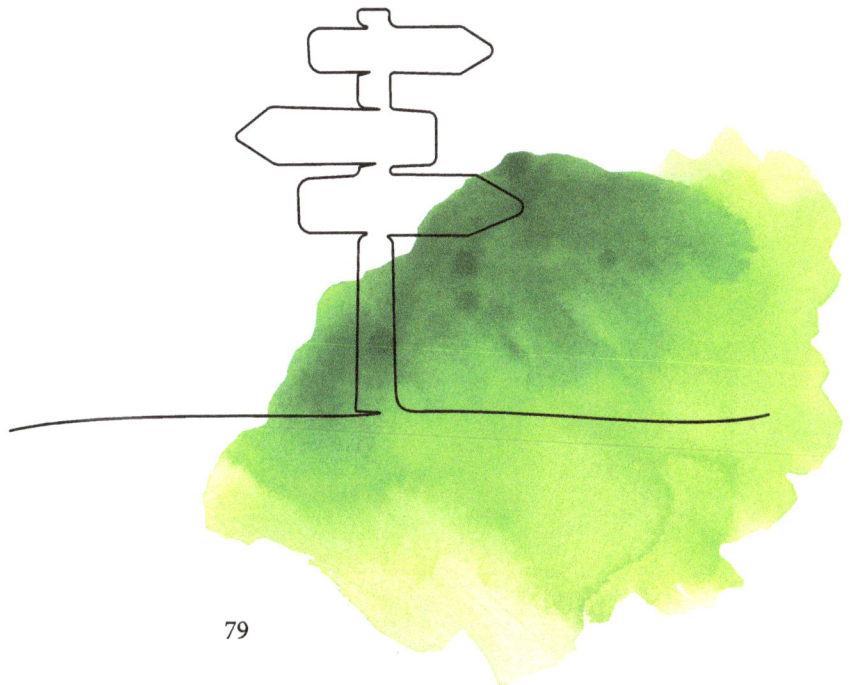

Seed

Encasing all it needs within itself

To grow exuberant and proud

With deep palpable extensions

The shift is imperceptible

Small touches forming surreptitiously

Its potential magically unleashed

Germinating when the synchronicity strikes

In a hidden flurry of unstoppable transformation

Guided by its sense of belonging

Displaying its uniqueness in full view

Bursting with admiration

Not a dew of abashed feeling

Laying the foundation

Upon which it settles

Belonging always to the earth

V

Pleasure and recreation

Self-expression

Romance

Organs and consciousness

Six senses

I drink

I drink
To pass
The time

I drink
Also
To enjoy

With others
I drink
And share

My own

I drink

As well

For sad

Moments

I drink

Happy

Ones too

I drink

Absorbed

So engaged in the task
Oblivious to what's around

Drive to work
Engrossed in thought

Don't recall how we made it
From the garage to the lot

Don't notice the red car in front
The motorcycle whizzing by

Body is present
Mind is making lists

Running through what happened
Envisioning what's next

So absorbed in conversation
The world fell away

Camera

Light and dark

Mark the speed

Manipulate depth

Center the eye

Square the focus

Crisp the highlight

Blur the back

Record posterity

In a snap

Hummingbird

Hover
And extract
In spurts of hues

Dashing
To and fro
Mining nectar

The bird
The typist
Racing the clock

Self-Expression

I dilly dally

Senseless explanations

Without diving into the tale

I feel the murkiness

Until I share the story

So, I do

Sending a wish

To meet on the other side

Ideas form into words

Shape written images

Lighting my imagination

A spark of creativity

Powerful motivation

To unleash

Self-expression

Leading me

To glow

Courage

Meant to express for a long time
It is something I kept
In the back of my mind

I didn't find the words
Definitely been afraid
I still am missing courage

I stopped letting it halt me
Threw caution to the wind
And took that step

It was just one
It made a big difference
To finally share

Strive

I live in cliches

Struggle

It's the power of words

Poignant

For years I resisted

Smile

My only fortress

Fake

Until I found words

Unburdened

So much distress

Impress

Regrets in the body

Soul

Plenty of pain

Lack

I carry words

Unspoken

Shame and guilt

Mute

When I didn't mean to

Failed

Words weighed heavily on me

Tense

Taking many chances

Travel

Learned lessons

Marvel

Started again

Against

Words of advice, odds, common sense

Strive

Follow my gut instinct

Spirit

The only way I found words

Intuition

Push away the nos

Doubt

Find the yesses

Grow

Openness

Even if it hurts

Stay open

Even when afraid

Stay open

Even in failure

Stay open

Even when criticized

Stay open

To experience life

Stay open

To fill with love

Stay open

To be joyful

Stay open

To feel excited

Stay open

No matter what

Stay open

VI

Health

Routine and work

Courage

Coming together as a whole

Develop personality and self-respect

Alerts

Thank you body
For alerting me
When I needed
To be more wholesome

For being my vessel
To live as I have
Loving me and caring
When I wasn't able

For putting up with
Laziness and abuse
Taking you for granted
Limits I pushed

For being my faithful companion
Through thick and thin
Growing and developing
Alongside my life

For handling changes

Exertion into exhaustion

Ebbs and flows

The down lows

For communicating with me

Prodding and poking

When I need redirection

Healing and resting

For being more connected

Than I am consciously capable

Knowing what is

Of my highest good

For teaching me

To listen and learn

From all that I have

All I have lived

Wellness

My rock and my core
Supporting me in ways
Beyond my awareness

Being patient
No matter what I put you through
Making sure I learned my lessons

Unexplainable illnesses
Explainable ones too
Brought on by stress

Springing back to life
When all hope was lost
Time and time again

A magic miracle pill
Hidden in your treasures
Just within reach

Knowing better than I did
What I needed most
To put myself together

Thank you body
For being exactly as you are
Finding a path to wellness

For your unconditional love
Making me aware
Of all that I am

Skin

Within me a wailing stirs
That will not be perceived

Other than for the anger
Piercing through my flesh

In a rashness of frustration
An itchiness of bitter

A fiery energy surging
Through every pore within me

It's not until I release
Detox from the negativity

That my largest organ soothes
Reaches a level of calm

That results in a smoothness
I've never seen before

Making the discomfort worthwhile
A new level of peace

Forcing

I mark my understanding of the world
In the midst of my skin burning
I review the many lessons learned

There is no point fighting
It only brings out more anger
More frustration

There is no point hiding
That only isolates me
And make up rubs off

There is no point sharing
It only brings unwanted attention
Unsolicited advice

Listening is the key

It brings understanding

I can only soothe and calm

Peace will evolve on its own

There is no point wondering how or why

Acceptance leads more quickly to a solution

It is happening

It simply is

There is no point forcing

Healing Miracles

Healing miracles
Brought to light

Not to fester and grow
More significant

Cease to dwell in the cavern
Not thriving on darkness

For in that darkness it grew
Bigger and ominous

Once in the light
It had nowhere to go

Shriveling up
Into a sweet raisin

Evidence I am better
Simply because

I brought it to light
A miracle of healing

Monotony

The screen play the same images

Every day is re-lived

Moments blend into themselves

One second indistinguishable from the next

The mirror reflects the same face

Skin has permanently paled

Blemishes go untouched

Where one goes another comes

The window displays the same view

Neighbors hop into their lives

Early morning cue it's time to rise

Masked kids walk as I sip my nourishment

There is no way to cope

When all we want is to be safe

Gain the courage to deftly slip away

Just to create a different kind of day

Time

Slave to

Time

Adhere to

Time

Ask for more

Time

Wish we had

Time

Yet

Time

Is a construct

Time

Can bend

Time

Can be prioritized

Time

Can be optimized

And

Time

Is a bond

Time

Passes in cycles

Time

Exists in space

Time

Is but an illusion

Moment

When undisturbed
The world turns to entropy
There is meaning in chaos
Disorder is how we thrive
How we find ways to survive

Forge our way forward
With no other resources
Than the courage on our backs
Perseverance on our shoulders
Gumption on our behinds

We work through challenges

Chip away at our lessons

Sculpting the obstacles

Finding our way through the fog

Clearing the thick foliage

Until we find a clearing

A place to move and breathe freely

Shake off the mold

To make sense of who we are

Finding magic in the moment

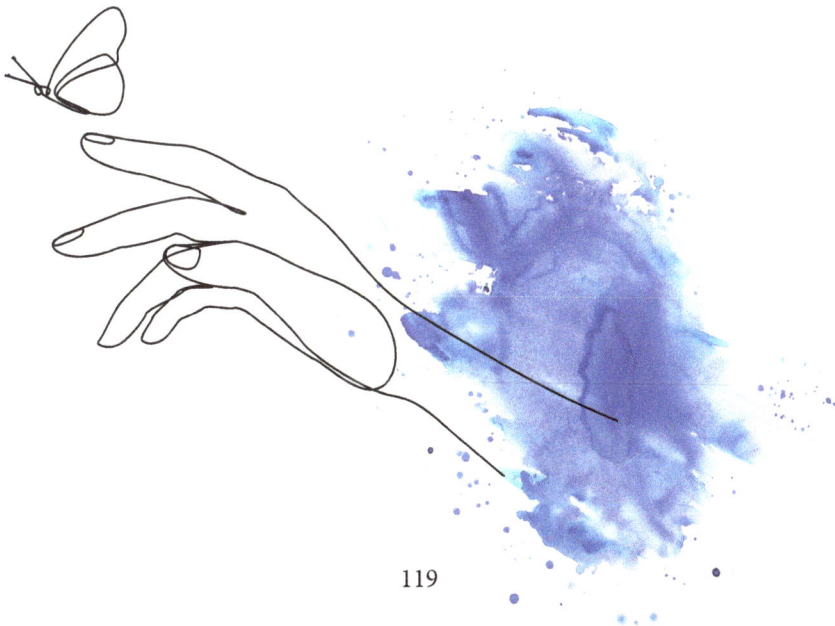

VII

Balance and equilibrium

All types of partnerships

Sensation of pleasure and pain

Limited choices

Dramatic feelings

Perfection

There is no such thing

There is no need

Especially not to be Goldilocks

Nothing is too easy or hard

Too small or big

It is perfect

Just the way it is

In all its crooked glory

Perfection is a construct

Not a reality

Matter

My life mattered

Not

Unless I was married

Another

A person who is supportive
Kind and generous

Giving love freely
Values of respect and trust

Wholly embraces all I give
And shares all they have

That doesn't take for granted
Just because we are meant to be

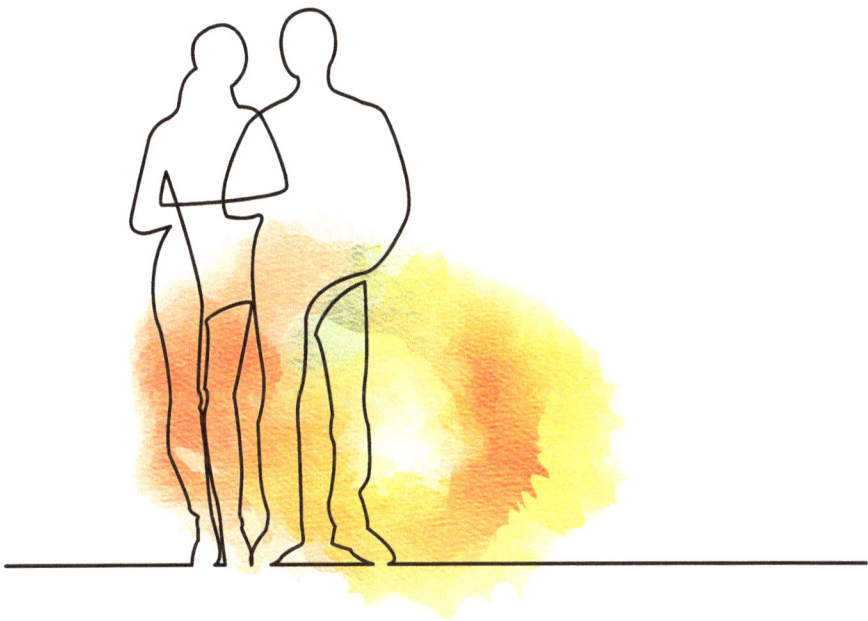

Miss you

Miss doesn't begin to encompass
What I feel

Webster says miss means
Feel absence

Webster can't explain what I feel
Nor can miss

Part of me is with you
Given happily

Part of you is with me
Maybe not purposefully

Adrift
Is how I feel

Webster says
Leaving out

I say incomplete
Without you

Hold hands

They walked down a path
In separate directions
Each thinking the same thought

There was a foot of snow on the ground
The air chilled below freezing
Warmth escaping from every pore

Bundled up tightly
Face aching in the frigid air
The solitary prospect

How perfect the night was
To walk home
With someone holding their hand

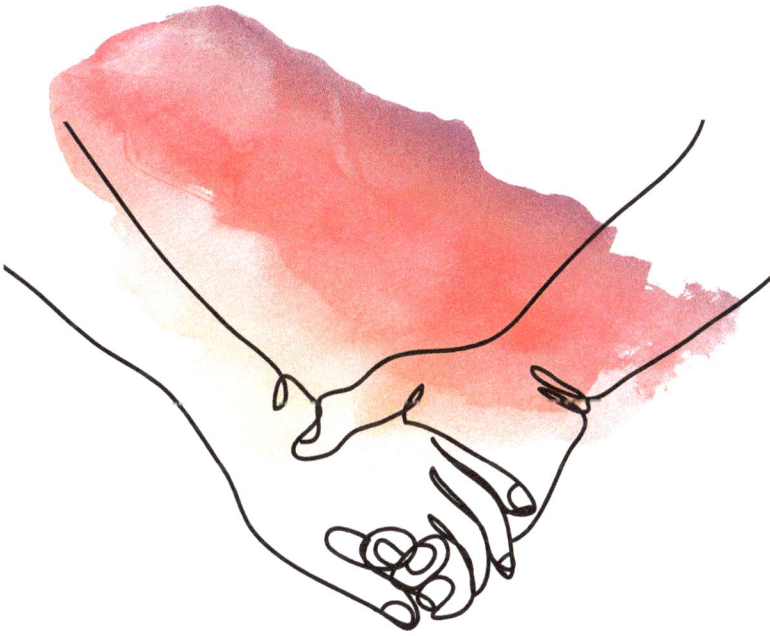

Two's

Two is for relationships
Soul mission
When the veil is thin
The intuitive feminine rises

Two is for balance
22, 2:22, 22:22
Signifying partnership
Cooperation

Two and twenty is a master number
Exert personal power
The ability to manifest
Making dreams come true

Two is better than one
We aren't meant for isolation
Rather collaboration
Togetherness

Homeostasis

A strive for balance
Within

Our bodies aim for it
For us

Habits and practices
Air it

Health and mindfulness
Have purpose

Even when we don't
Body acts

Signals we need to pivot
Aid it

To blissfully reach
Balance

Mandala

A spiritual depiction

As above so within

As below so without

An intricate connection

Metered circular steps

Cycles that perpetuate

Designs that collapse

Were a single slice removed

The aim is always the same

Put us back together

In glorious harmony

VIII

Transformation

Cycles of birth and death

Desire to hold on to pleasure

Separate from pain

Self-indulgence

Frost

In the morning I wake

A thick sheen upon the earth

A frozen layer conceals

A wakening underground

As winter quietly vanishes

Not yet showing signs

Of the new life

About to spring forward

Change

The air is thick
Smells of impending rain

Leaves rustling on leaves
Flutters are electric

Horses prick their ears
Earth sends silent rumbles

Grays tumble in the horizon
A hurricane appears lurking

Daring souls emerge
Pets hurry to keep pace

Skin tenses in goosebumps
Butterflies on rapid fire

A tangible transcendence
Only a matter of time

Karma

I thought this was part of my life

Not just that I deserved it

But that it was a part of me

I didn't quite understand

Why it would be so

Having not done anything terribly bad

I thought it was my lot in life

My luck of the draw

The short end of the stick

In a later life

Or ones before

It had likely been different

But in this one

What I got

I needed to accept

Everything happens

Even if we're not sure

What the reason is

A karmic retribution

Hurts caused in past lives

Or a lesson for later in life

All I thought was

This is how it was destined

Veiled in sadness

It didn't occur to me

Pull myself out

Create new prospects

I had within my reach

The power to heal

Feel joy and happiness

Acknowledgement

Life changes

It hurts to be left

At a loss

Grief encroaches

Change is difficult

Acknowledgement provides release

Don't justify how you feel

Allowing to simply feel

Trying to pave our way

Make the best with what we got

Cope with loneliness

Dreams that don't come true

And soon

Chaos settles

Entropy stands still

The road comes into view

Pathways can be discerned

We see the next step

A parting in the clouds

Lets in a ray of sun

That is all it takes

To make a difference

To bring hope

Feeling it's possible

A brightening on the horizon

On the curvy journey

Life changes

Results in beauty

Radical turnaround

I am in the midst
Of a 180

Except
I didn't go anywhere

I may have gone backwards
A bit

Needed the leverage
In my step

Before I took a chance
To turn a U

The days had grown bleak
Boring

I had to face my reality
Broken

I had reached a wall
Stalled

No where else to go
I felt

Hired a construction team
Repaired

Rebuild
Putting back the pieces

Within
Time is in my hands

I am letting go of so much
Feels absolute

Outsiders no longer come
Before me

All they had to do
Was be

All I had to do
Was please

I needed that
They needed me

I tipped it over
I come first

It's the only way
To move forward

Not to slog away
At life

Now what
The thought distracts me

Where do I go
With this new orientation

Which oyster do I take
World

Eating would be more fun
Satisfying

For that I need strength
Direction

And a narrowing of dreams
Or an expansion

With this radical turnaround
New chances

A new found resolve
Intentions

I can finally get back
To living

This existence has more
Possibility

On my terms
Empowered

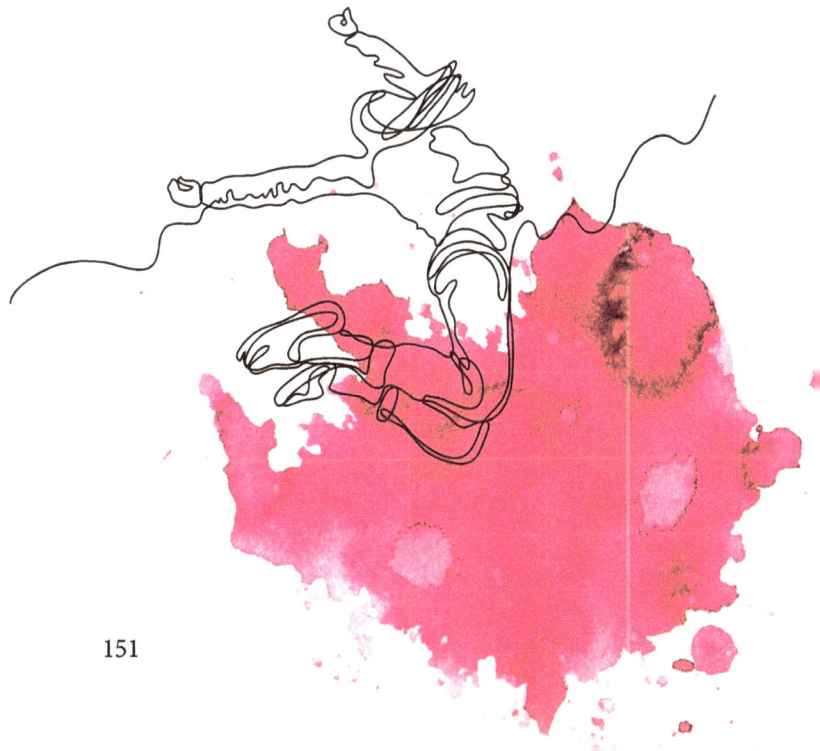

Liminal

The time hasn't come yet to act
Pause for the right conditions
Stuck in a place I didn't want
The best location for the moment

The time hasn't come yet to move
So much needs to be set in motion
Jabs and stabs to be settled
Waiting in turn for my moment

The time hasn't come yet to travel
The passport itching to get stamped
So many places to cross off the list
Waiting for pause in the moment

The time hasn't come yet
It will come, it's a matter of time
For conditions to be set right
To cease the moment

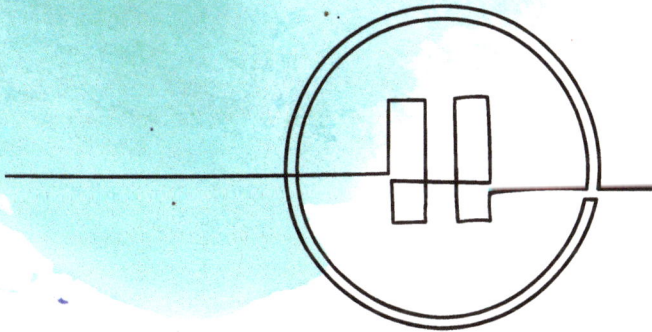

Death

My Tarot card

Is the death card

Number XIII

The grim reaper

Without a scythe

Doesn't always come for death

I knocked on death's door

A few times

A plane crashed

A tumble that crippled

A collapsed lung

It wasn't my time

Allow the storm to wash through

Shake off the dust

Reconstitute and recreate

Breathe fresh air

Approach life differently

Look from a new perspective

A chance to pivot and redirect

Overcome obstacles and challenges

Start again with a different view

Makeshift

Revealing a morphing

However many times it took

The universe prods

Until you pay attention

Pay I did

There was no one else but me

Rising up again

Leaving ashes behind

Turning over leaves

Like pages in a printed book

Everything growing stronger

Standing more confident

Not dying in my skin

Immortal

Dying

I've never feared
Dying

Wishing only I pass after
My loves

I don't welcome
It

I simply know it will come
One day

Meanwhile I make the most of life
Trying

Not to take moments for granted
Or people

Bowing my head in gratitude
For blessings

Know that when my times comes
I am ready

For only I will change
In form

My soul will move on
Not die

Living in another form
Forever

IX

Purpose

Exploration

Do things as you feel

Grasping and clinging to what's pleasant

Spirituality

Outlook

Three words conveying
Significant deep messages
Guidance meaning motivation

Creating light inspiration
Insightful profound transmission
Faithfully trust purpose

Welcome giving freely
Listening blooms feeling
Grace compassion kindness

Clearly respectful energetic
Stand strong peacock
Confidently strutting honor

Positive chilling peaceful
Strong sunny graceful
Embracing magic grateful

Life path

May you follow
Your life path

Follow what feels good
In your heart

That's all we need
For meaning

To matter
You must just be

Purpose comes
Following what feels right

Purpose

We are meant
Walk gracefully upon earth
Barely making an impact

Live a life of purpose
Leave it better than we found it
Make a difference

Yet we amount to nothing
Wads of collected stardust
Barely making it through the day

Living a life of monotony
Unable to see the difference
Day by day

It's doing something we love
That brings a smile
Even if just to one person

It makes a difference
That ripples unseen
Touching someone else

That's how it spreads
Person to person
Showing our lives matter

A drive

Gazing out
I observe
Curious not engaging

A passing vehicle
A blip on the radar
A one-time flash that barely registers

I don't engage
I don't roll down the window
I don't wave

Simply carry on
An eager spectator
Merely carrying on

For a moment I wonder

Where they are going

And why

The wonder passes

New scenery and people

New thoughts

Where we are headed

Why we are

All on this road

Go beyond

Go beyond
Push
Expand

Go beyond limits
Push comfort
Expand dreams

Go beyond fears
Push beliefs
Expand thoughts

Go beyond expectations
Push assumptions
Expand ideas

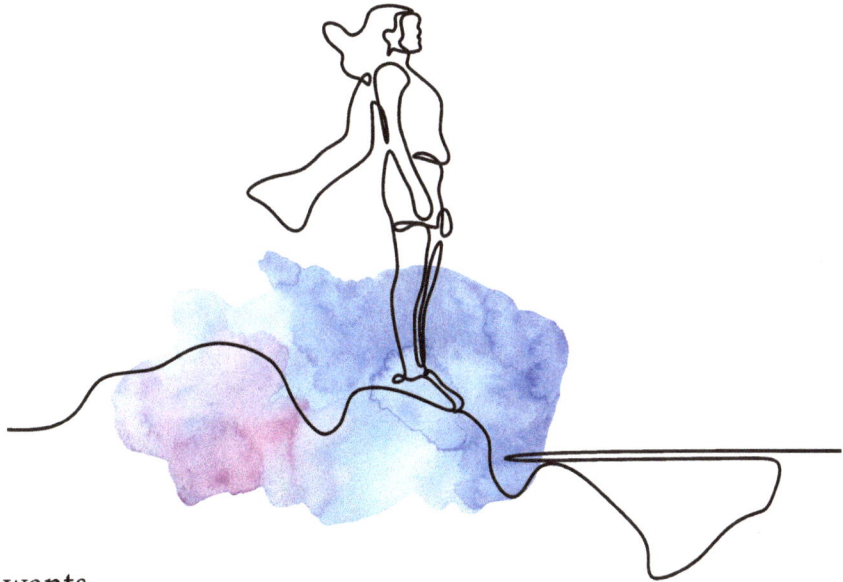

Go beyond wants

Push needs

Expand desires

Go beyond

And push

And expand

Be limitless

Be infinite

Be one

Now

Everything makes sense

I feel at peace

I feel what I am meant to feel

I experience what I am meant to experience

There is perfection in the moment

Even when I don't sense it

Everything is as it should

No matter how scattered it all seems

Absence

I had a feeling
A message would come
It was a sense
I brushed off
Wishful thinking

Then I got it
That message
It made me feel
All the feels
A full heart

Seemed like a thought
A memory perhaps
Not from presence
Reaching out
But from absence

Divine entourage

What does that mean

Do what feels right

Quiet the mind and body

Intent on hearing the internal flutters

Follow my inner guidance

When I breathe with ease

I proceed

When I don't I cease

Be of service to others

A pillar of generosity

Doesn't require I give myself away

Simple acts of kindness and compassion

Include myself

I cannot truly love another

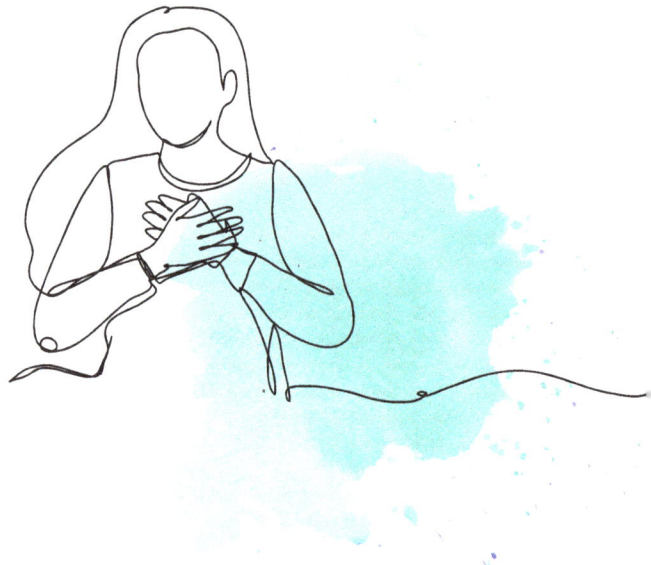

Until I feel wholeness within

To step into my power
I don't bend my will
I light my fire

It feels good
Because it doesn't infringe
On another

It gives us all wings

We all feel that light
Wishing
Recognize it in each other

Honoring we are connected
Bringing us closer
Through this divine entourage

X

Enterprise

Making a mark

Achievement

Becoming & existence

Tremendous awareness

Streaming

Stream
In daylight
Instead of company
And at night
To drown
Silence

Entertaining
For weeks
But after months
It is senseless
To listlessly
Watch

Distraction
Is hard
In this climate
It is hard
To find
Peace

Ambition

Eyes set high

High in the sky

Sky stretching out

Out far in

In to the horizon

Horizon reaching to infinity

Infinity that's endless

Endless with possibility

Capricorn

The most ambitious

Of the twelve

No matter how high

We climb up and up

To get what we want

No mountain too high

No slope too steep

Crushing obstacles

Within our reach

How come is it

That I don't feel

Like a true

Capricorn

Achievement

Bopped from here to there
Been to yonder and wonder

Tried frights and delights
Sampled wear and tear

Practiced crimps and shifts
Polished heaves and weaves

Experienced shapes and shakes
Checked off too many a rock and box

Amalgamated into strife and life
Right into who I am that I am

What is meant

Come together
Follow our heart's call

There's no other way
To live life without

Regrets or negative thoughts
That life was meant

To be lived otherwise
Than as it is

Embracing

Everything that created me
Embracing my health

Everything that plagued and saved me
Embracing my life

Everything that led me here
Embracing my past

Everything that guided me
Embracing my future

Everything I thought and felt
Embracing my self

Everything I did and acted
Embracing my highest good

Knock

I knocked on a door for a novel
And the door for poetry opened
Unexpected

Sometimes that's how it works
We just have to stay open
Surprise

Knock on one door
A different one opens
Unexpected

An opportunity presented that wouldn't have

If we didn't knock on the first door

Surprise

Leads down a path

Resulting in a series of other events

Unexpected

An initiative

And an open mind

Surprise

All we needed was to knock

One small act

Unexpected

Create

We can manifest

What we want to create

I bring into my vortex

What I want to feel

Calling to the stars

With every breath

Pulsating like a whish in space

The light of a constellation

Shining as part of the galaxy

Making sure I know

In its every twinkle

I have access granted

To all I need

All I dream

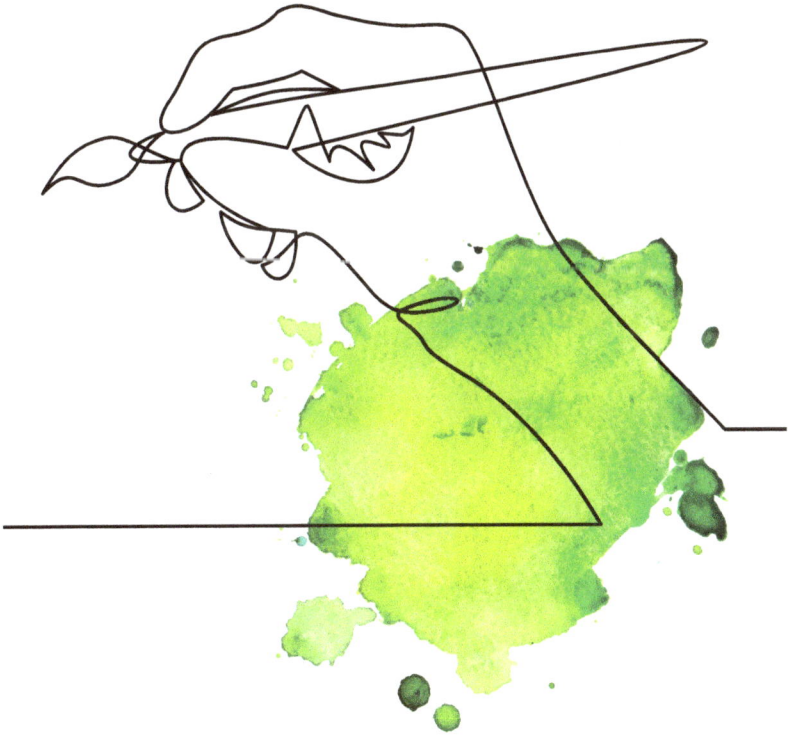

XI

Blessings

Support & connectedness

Hopes & wishes

Conception of next life

Strong vitality

Friendship

There is beauty in growth
Mature, travel, and work
Marry and have kids
Priorities and responsibilities shift

There is beauty in bonds
Gatherings grow less frequent
New relations form
Past ones a nostalgic memory

There is beauty in connection
People come into our lives
Creating cherished memories
Soul marking stages in time

There is beauty in beginnings

And so in endings

Life creates those coming and going

Each just right for the particular moment

There is beauty in friendship

None diminished because of separation

Nor more important because they are ancient or fresh

Happening exactly when we need them

Constant

Thank you for making
This unique year
Not just bearable
But more enjoyable

I felt connected
Despite the isolation
Looked forward to our calls
No matter how much we struggled

You gave me light
Amidst the monotony
Of the groundhog-like days
Long silent hours

Thank you
For your constant friendship
The virtual hugs
The eternal love

Patronize

Frequent

Like a customer

Apparently kind

While feeling

Superior

Really

A put down

Like they know better

Like I am naive

Blank

Too dull or stupid

To figure it out

Without their expert

Guidance and input

Unassuming

But that doesn't mean

I let you stroke

Your ego

On my behalf

Perhaps

It helps to observe

From a distance

Without letting myself

Be pulled in

Sucked

Entitled you are

To your view and opinion

And me to mine

Blank is right

Me

Hurt

Hurt people hurt
I keep that in mind
Every time I hear
A word that's unkind

It helps me feel empathy
For the one who was rude
I try not to take personally
No matter how crude

I observe from a distance
Their hurt comes from pain
Something unrelated
To the moment we gain

Instead I try to see

All they need is compassion

A kindness perhaps

That has yet to get traction

I extend a silent nod

Maybe a smile

That keeps me at bay

Removing myself in style

No longer feeds a spirit

Who only needs love

Perhaps even a hug

Fit into my life like a glove

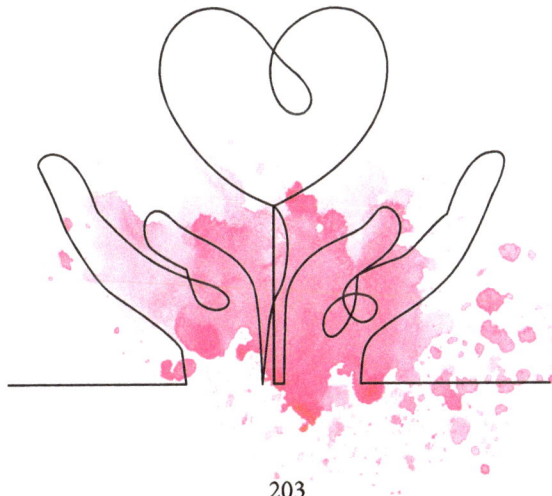

Something

Everybody has
A thing or many
Something

A worry an ache a pain
An emptiness
Something

A story they have not told
Something
They've held back

Not wanting to be judged

For something

Or shunned

Pretending to grin

At something

Not a hair out of place

Hiding the anguish

Despair

Or something

If only we knew we all have

Something

We share

Cutting cords

I lie awake

My eyes rest closed

The night is still

Everyone lies chill

But me

Thoughts plague me

Worries circle through the night

Waking me every hour

On the hour

Leaching away my dreams

One by one

I identify every notion

That pokes at my ease

Draining my peace

Clinging for one moment longer

I search for

Energetic scissors

Sever the connection

Invoke a cloak of protection

Enveloping me in calm

Happiness

Happiness is not something you pursue

It is something you choose

It's that simple, not easy

What about the lies, loss, misery, and cruelty

Or the time our hearts were ripped out of our chest

Was it really a choice

Step into freedom

A break from chains that hold us

Happiness comes when we stop

What about worries, fears, confusion, and frustration

Or headaches, taxes, and wallowing

Choose to let it slip away

Give in and surrender

Choose to be happy

Regardless of tomorrow or the day after

Shit happened

Is happening

Will continue to happen

That's life

Choose

Despite it all

Choose now, this moment

It's all we have

Be happy

Hope

The moment before a sneeze

Breath is suspended

Impending with relief

The horizon is on the rise

Promise of an imposing twilight

Tantalizing streaks of purple, orange, yellow

The pause feels liminal

Record of the anticipation

Trusting in what is to come

XII

Sacrifice

Rehabilitation

Self-undoing

Intuition

Aging, decay, and feebleness

White hair

I used to get one a year

A single white hair

Mocking me

I plucked it

Wiped clean

As if it never was

Until another appeared

Again the next year

I denied it

This year I halted

Plucking

All my whites

My denial

Disabled

Not wanting to go bald

Fear

Cast away your fears
I was told
Ignore

They are all I have
Leech my dreams
Awake

Squeeze my emotions
Knuckles turn white
Crack

Burst the floodgates
Sob until dry
Gasp

Lost in emptiness
Turn to nothing
Surrender

In the calm
Sense the unknown
Love

It's always been there
See it
Feel

It's who I am
Shape my essence
Trust

Stuck

Something comes up
No matter how big or small
Deep or shallow
Entrenched or recent
Let it go

Not letting it go feeds fear
Fear keeps us stuck
Blocked
Feeding anger
Envy, jealousy, and competition

Work with the heart
Keep it open
The energy moving
Releasing stagnation
Ugliness unleashed

We need not summon it

Deny or cling

Avoid or reject

Grab or block

When it shows up

See it

Touch it

Feel it

Acknowledge it

But don't follow it

Smile at it

Welcome it

Embrace it

Accept and let go

Gently send it on its way

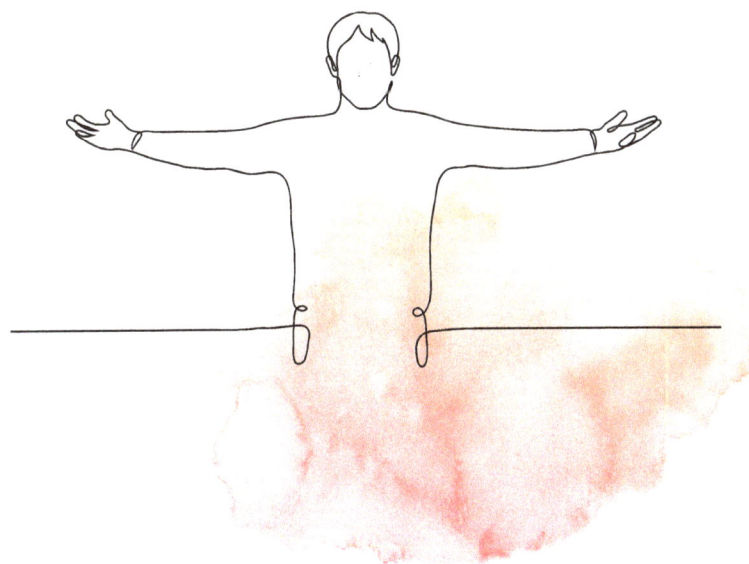

Anger

I feel it so often

These days

Living in these constraints

I had no choice

None of us did

Aren't we all

In the same place

And isn't there

So much else

I live with

We live with

That we can choose

So I shift

Not indulging it

A crack

A crack likes to slip
Easy to miss

A subtle twitch of the eyelid
Tear that doesn't drop

A slight tremble in a smile
Meek contortion of the face

A weight between words
Loneliness clothed in appearance

A look lost in the flight of a bird
Missed thread in conversation

A pause before an answer
Echo of silence

A hand that craves compassion
Skin yearns for soft touch

A life may feel different
Pain looks the same

Clinging

Thoughts are passing
Fleeting images
In the space of my mind

Fleeting they would be if I did not want to look closer
Fleeting they would be if I did not examine
Fleeting they would be if I did not crave for the despair

Fleeting they cease to be
Images that mesmerize
I cling

I cling to interpret and find explanations
I cling to justify and come up with excuses
I cling to criticize and self-deprecate

I cling to blame

I cling to judge

I cling to convict

I cling because it seems better than now

I cling because it clarifies the now

I cling because it shows why I feel empty

But if I were truly empty

Don't I at least have what I am clinging to?

How then can I be empty?

A thought passes

I cling again

But this time I notice

I realize I am clinging

I realize I don't need to

I realize I can loosen my grip

Finger by finger
One by one
And fully let go

I am free again
Cherishing the emptiness of the moment
Until the next passing thought

I want to cling once again
Except this time
Maybe I don't

Freedom takes work
When we let go we are truly empty
We are truly free

Re-start

I noticed a scrape on my elbow

Same one on the other side

Not quite mirror images

One darker and more bothersome

What I had done I couldn't place

The cause I couldn't name

Lathering on an ointment

A thick salve I placed

Rubbed it while I counted to twenty

For good measure

For the moisture to seep

With tender loving strokes

Day after day I nourished
Twice or thrice as needed
And pressing on I did
Bandaging on occasion

Persistence brought in moisture
Removing the dry flaky flesh
Making space for a fresh one
To grow in its place

All there is

Without what has come into our lives
We wouldn't have grown

We had to see we're not less than
Being taken for granted wasn't a right

No one is entitled to another
People can't use as they please

Life doesn't occur on human terms
We are pushed until we crack open

Accept grace and mercy
Let in healing

Learn forgiveness and compassion
To spread the healing

We have what we need inside us
All of us do

Through the doubt and despair
The laughter and delight

What we need is within
We are all there is

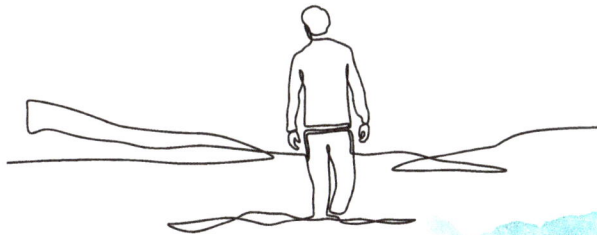

Thank you to every single reader. You motivate me to write.

Thank you to Karen for continuing to make magic happen. I am in awe of who you are because you help me believe that anything is possible. You gave me the wings I needed to fly.

Thank you to Jennifer for the beautiful cover.

Thank you to Ida for your gorgeous designs. They elevated me beyond the skies.

Some of the poems in this book have been taken from or adapted from those I posted on social media. Thank you to every person who liked, hearted, commented and/or shared one of the poems I posted. It was scary to start posting so publicly, yet you made me feel I had the wings to fly.

Thank you to my parents and brother for believing in me. You gave me the encouragement to take flight.

About the Author

Sonee Singh is a cross-cultural seeker of deep knowing. She writes stories of self-discovery to encourage people to accept themselves for who they are and live life on their own terms. Her tales are of her character's definitive moments on their life's journey. The mystical and spiritual are integral in her storytelling, as is her multi-cultural background.

Sonee is of Indian descent, born in Mexico, raised in Colombia, and resides in the United States. When not traveling, reading, or writing, she indulges in meditation, yoga, and aromatherapy.

She holds a Bachelor of Arts in Biology and Society and a Master of Management in Hospitality from Cornell University, and a Master of Science in Complementary Alternative Medicine from American College of Healthcare Sciences. She is currently pursuing a Doctor of Divinity from the University of Metaphysical Sciences.

She worked in hospitality before practicing as a wellness coach. She is certified as an Integrative Nutrition Health Coach, International Certified Health Coach, Reiki Master, Registered Aromatherapist™, Certified Crystal Energy Guide, Certified in Advanced Angel Card Master, and intuitive. These certifications feature in her writing.

Sonee has published her first book in a collection of poetry: *Embody.* She has also been published in two anthologies: *Blessing the Page* and *The Colours of Me.* She has multiple articles published on *Elephant Journal.*

Follow her on **www.soneesingh.com**

www.ingramcontent.com/pod-product-compliance
Lightning Source LLC
Chambersburg PA
CBHW060756150426
42811CB00058B/1422